NO-BULLYING PROGRAM

PREVENTING BULLYING AT SCHOOL

TEACHER'S MANUAL
FOR GRADES 2 AND 3

JAMES BITNEY, CURRICULUM WRITER

BEVERLY B. TITLE, Ph.D., PROGRAM DEVELOPER

HAZELDEN®

JOHNSON INSTITUTE

Hazelden
Center City, Minnesota 55012-0176
1-800-328-9000
1-651-213-4590 (Fax)
www.hazelden.org

First published by Johnson Institute–QVS, Inc., 1996

(Original edition titled *No-Bullying Program,
Preventing Bully/Victim Violence at School: Teacher's Manual for Grades 2 and 3*)

Revised edition published by Hazelden, 2001
Printed in the United States of America

ISBN 1-56838-731-8

Acknowledgments
The contents of this book are based on the No-Bullying Curriculum model originally developed
for the St. Vrain Valley School District, Longmont, Colorado, by Beverly B. Title, Ph.D.,
with assistance from Lisa Anderson-Goebel, Vivian Bray, K. G. Campanella-Green,
Ted Goodwin, Karen Greene, Elizabeth Martinson, Mike O'Connell, and Peggy Stortz.

The Bullying Behavior Chart was developed by Beverly B. Title, Ph.D.; Severance Kelly, M.D.;
Louis Krupnik, Ed.D.; Joseph Matthews, M.S.W.; Sue Kelsall, M.S.W.; and Kendra Bartley, M.A.

Curriculum consultation was provided by Peggy O'Connell.

05 04 03 02 01   6 5 4 3 2

Logo design by David Spohn
Cover design by David Spohn
Text design and typesetting by Spaulding & Kinne
Artwork by Sally Brewer Lawrence

Contents

Introduction

School Zones—Danger Zones

Violent incidents happen in our schools. They happen on the school buses. They happen on the playgrounds. They happen in school lunchrooms. They happen in the rest rooms. They happen in the hallways where students move from class to class. And they happen in the classroom, disrupting teachers from teaching and students from learning.

According to the National Education Association, each day many thousands of U.S. students skip school to avoid danger; others steer clear of the hallways, rest rooms, or school grounds; some students switch schools because of safety concerns, while others carry weapons for self-protection. Teachers and other school staff are also targeted. These professionals have had their property damaged or stolen, and they are threatened and physically attacked in the places they work.

Violence threatens the fiber of our education system. In some schools, gunfights have replaced fistfights, and students practice bullet drills in addition to fire drills. In recent years, schools have been the setting for violent incidents so extreme that they have received international news coverage. As the 1990s came to a close, the names of communities where students killed classmates and school staff were etched into our collective memory as nationwide we extended our hearts to the residents of Pearl, Mississippi; West Paducah, Kentucky; Jonesboro, Arkansas; Edinboro, Pennsylvania; Fayetteville, Tennessee; Springfield, Oregon; Littleton, Colorado; Conyers, Georgia; Deming, New Mexico; and Fort Gibson, Oklahoma. Then, in February 2000, at the dawn of the twenty-first century, a first-grader in Mount Morris Township, Michigan, shot and killed his classmate. We've also heard tragic reports from rural, suburban, and urban communities across the United States of students who have committed suicide when they can no longer take the verbal and physical abuse other students have directed at them.

1

Although schools sometimes seem to be worlds unto themselves, what happens in elementary, middle, and high schools is a reflection of what's going on in the broader culture. Certain trends in youth violence are of great concern to educators. One such trend is the increased lethality of youth violence. It's not so much that the percentage of youth committing crimes has increased, but that the nature of the crimes committed has worsened. An incident that led to an assault in years past might now end in homicide. The threat "I'm going to punch your lights out" has become "I'm going to blow your head off." The crimes youth are committing have become more deadly.

Another trend, related to the increase in the lethality of youth violence, is that weapons are appearing more frequently in schools. Even more disturbing is the fact that much younger children are bringing them. Years ago, in our discussions of the presence of guns at school, educators used to assume that only high school students would carry guns. Then we began to consider middle schools in that same conversation. Now educators have to consider elementary school children when we're voicing our concerns about guns at school because even the youngest students have brought in guns.

Another trend is that females are increasingly committing violent crimes. "Although male juveniles still account for the vast majority of violent offenses, the proportion of violent crimes committed by females is increasing at a faster rate than those of males, according to an FBI study."[1] According to the Justice Department's Office of Juvenile Justice and Delinquency Prevention, between 1992 and 1996, the number of girls arrested for violent crimes increased 25 percent, while there was no increase in the number of arrests of young men for the same crimes.[2]

Perhaps an outgrowth of the other trends is the response of those who have traditionally been called crime victims (today, many of these individuals prefer to be called "survivors" rather than "victims"). They are standing up for their rights. In the United States, a national movement has emerged that argues the unfairness of the fact that only criminals have rights under the Constitution: the rights of the accused. As a result of the persistent efforts of survivors of crime, most states have passed victim's rights amendments, and it's predicted to be only a matter of time before a victim's rights amendment is added to the U.S. Constitution. The importance of this movement is evident in light of discovering that, preceding several of

---

1. Lindsay Wise, "Violent Young Women Growing Societal Woe," *Denver Rocky Mountain News,* 9 July 1999, 50A.

2. Ibid.

the most extreme incidents of school violence, the perpetrators had been chronically bullied at school. In perpetrating violence with guns, they attempted to change the power imbalance that becomes established in a bullying situation.

When we look at the trends in school violence, we realize that we can no longer safely assume that students won't use extreme violence. We can no longer safely assume that even our youngest students won't use weapons. We can no longer safely assume that girls won't engage in physical violence, and we can no longer safely assume that the "tough" kids are the only threat to students and school staff. Too many students and school staff use violence, witness violence, or are the targets of violence.

Examining cultural trends in youth violence is enlightening; however, they don't capture the full picture of the violent incidents that occur in schools. Educators have overlooked many types of violence, forms of violence that contribute to the high-level violence captured in these trends. Often dismissed as "kids being kids," these violent behaviors—bullying behaviors—can affect a person throughout his or her lifetime. Firsthand reports bring home these effects in a powerful way. In late 1995, "Mindworks," a monthly forum for young readers in the Minneapolis *Star Tribune,* asked youth to respond to this question:

> Have you or anyone you know ever been teased, bullied, or harassed? Have you ever teased, bullied, or harassed anyone? Why do children and teens behave this way? What can teachers and other adults do to help?

The responses the paper received from children reveal the fear and hurt experienced by the targets of the violent behavior of children who bully:

> When I get teased, it makes me feel sad. Sometimes I feel like I'm in a world with only bullies and no friends *(rural sixth-grader).*

> I've been bullied before and it isn't fun. My knees were shaking and it was scary, like you just want to cry for your mommy or put [the bully] in jail *(urban third-grader).*

> Adults just don't seem to understand what it feels like to be teased. If they did, they wouldn't act like it's okay. When somebody teases you, it feels like they just punched you in the stomach *(suburban fifth-grader).*

The newspaper received more than 12,000 such responses from students of all ages, and from all types of communities—12,000! As these firsthand accounts point out, many children view school as a daily gauntlet of violence that they are forced to face.

Violence: A Definition

To begin to change schools from places where students and staff members fear their safety, it's crucial for school staff to first reach agreement on just what behaviors we consider violent. Unfortunately, *violence* means different things to different people. As educators, we need a clear definition of *violence* that helps us to set boundaries for students' behavior and leaves no room for ambivalence or individual interpretation of which incidents are violent. Once defined, we can use the definition as a tool for prevention and intervention, enabling us to clarify for students what behaviors are unacceptable. That is why the *No-Bullying Program* suggests that educators consider using the following simple definition of violence:

> **Violence is any word, look, sign, or act that hurts a person's body, feelings, or things.**

This definition, which is also used in *Respect & Protect®*—a Hazelden/Johnson Institute school curriculum (see Resources)—is purposefully broad. It deliberately includes behaviors, like joking or teasing, that many of us consider to be fairly normal or innocent. We include such behaviors in the definition because we recognize that they have the potential to cause real emotional damage and lead to physical harm.

Included within this broad definition of *violence* are two important, distinct categories of violence: peer violence and bullying.

- Peer violence is defined as acts of violence that stem from disagreements, misunderstandings, or conflicting desires between students who are equally matched in power, which may be physical strength, social skill, verbal ability, or another resource.

- Bullying occurs whenever someone uses his or her power unfairly and repeatedly to hurt someone.

To make our schools safe and violence-free, school staff must intervene when they see either type of violence. Schools can successfully deal with the problem of peer violence by helping children grow in their knowledge and ability to use social skills such as communication, processing feelings, problem solving, conflict management,

4

and conflict mediation. Unfortunately, few schools have been successful in addressing bullying. We've designed the *No-Bullying Program* to provide schools with an educational model to address bullying that's based on research.

The *No-Bullying Program:* A Systemwide Approach to Addressing Bullying at School

Schools that rely on teaching social skills to students who bully as their sole measure to stem bullying probably won't see a change in their school climate. Students who bully don't respond as readily as most students to social skills work. They don't care that their actions create problems for others. In fact, they generally enjoy the results of their bullying behavior. Until students who bully have external incentive to adopt new behaviors, they will continue to engage in bullying behaviors. To get this population's attention, we must apply strict and consistent consequences.[3] Only at that point will efforts at teaching social skills to students who bully succeed.

Bullying at school is a systemic problem. When bullying occurs in a school, the problem extends beyond those who are directly involved in the violent incidents. Children who bully and targeted children make up approximately 15 percent of any school population.[4] The remaining 85 percent of the students are relatively uninvolved in bullying behaviors.

This doesn't mean, however, that bullying has no impact on the vast majority of students. The effects of bullying tend to ripple. If adults at school tolerate bullying, everyone becomes affected. Tolerance leads to entitlement, which means that students who engage in bullying feel that they are entitled—or have the right—to continue such behavior. The ripple effect of tolerance can be observed when students who might not otherwise act violently pick up on the unspoken message that violent behavior is tolerated. This leads them to perceive that they have *permission* to become violent.

As a teacher, you'll lead students through an exciting, educational process designed to empower them to put a stop to bullying and to make school a safe zone that is conducive to learning. The *No-Bullying Program* curriculum that you'll deliver is designed to generate willingness among targeted students and witnesses of bullying and encourage them to put a stop to bullying at school.

---

3. Dan Olweus, Ph.D., *Bullying at School: What We Know and What We Can Do* (Cambridge, Mass.: Blackwell Publishers, 1993), 67.

4. Ibid., 13.

This can be done by helping students do the following:

- define bullying and understand what behaviors are considered bullying

- understand the effect of bullying behaviors and develop empathy for targeted students

- learn ways to respond to bullying behavior

- learn when and how to report bullying

- learn the consequences the school has established for engaging in bullying behavior

To ensure that your school generates student support for the *No-Bullying Program,* the program also insists that all school staff members take a proactive role in dealing with bullying behavior. Researchers Debra J. Pepler and Wendy Craig from York University in Toronto, Canada, claim that if a student doesn't deflect the aggression of a child who bullies during the first incident, a pattern of behavior may become established.[5] At that point, adult intervention is required to put an end to the abuse. When children realize that, upon receiving student reports of bullying behavior, school staff will intervene immediately and follow through in enforcing consequences, they feel secure in turning to them for help.

Prior to delivering the curriculum to students, the program director will arrange a training during which all members of the school staff will become familiar with the *No-Bullying Program* and will discuss the policies and procedures the school is developing as part of implementing the program. Following are some important areas of discussion that the program director will cover:

- an overview of the research on bullying, including its impact on students not directly involved in bullying incidents, and of the philosophy and procedures the *No-Bullying Program* uses to reduce bullying behaviors in school

- how school staff members can often unwittingly enable bullying behavior

- the school's comprehensive strategy statement regarding bullying

- the school's consequence plan for students who engage in bullying behaviors

- the school's procedure for reporting bullying behaviors

- how to help students feel safe when they report bullying incidents

---

5. Debra J. Pepler and Wendy Craig, interview by Oprah Winfrey, *The Oprah Show,* Harpo, 14 Nov. 1997.

- how the school will evaluate the effectiveness of the program

- who will deliver the curriculum to the students and an overview of the teaching materials

During the overview of research on bullying behavior, you'll learn that bullying behaviors can be physical, emotional, or social, and can be verbal or nonverbal. The Bullying Behavior Chart on the next page will help you identify bullying behaviors.

Bullying behaviors include not only physical aggression, but also emotional harassment and social alienation. Each of the three major types of bullying—physical, emotional, and social—can be further split into verbal and nonverbal behaviors. Each of the six categories of bullying behavior exists along a continuum from low-level violence to more severe violence. The *No-Bullying Program* uses this chart to show the range and scope of bullying behaviors that can occur at school.

Bullying Behavior Chart

LEVELS	PHYSICAL Harm to another's body or property		EMOTIONAL Harm to another's self-worth		SOCIAL Harm to another's group acceptance	
	verbal	nonverbal	verbal	nonverbal	verbal	nonverbal
1	Taunting Expressing physical superiority	Making threatening gestures Defacing property Pushing / shoving Taking small items from others	Insulting remarks Calling names Teasing about possessions, clothes Saying someone has germs or is unclean	Giving dirty looks Holding nose or other insulting gestures	Gossiping Starting / spreading rumors Teasing publicly about clothes, looks, etc.	Passively not including in group Playing mean tricks
2	Threatening physical harm Blaming targeted student	Damaging property Stealing Initiating fights Scratching Tripping or causing a fall Assaulting	Insulting family Harassing with phone calls Insulting intelligence, athletic ability, etc.	Defacing schoolwork Falsifying schoolwork Defacing personal property, clothing, etc.	Insulting race, gender Increasing gossip / rumors Undermining other relationships	Making someone look foolish Excluding from the group
3	Making repeated and/or graphic threats Practicing extortion Making threats to secure silence: "If you tell, I will . . ."	Destroying property Setting fires Biting Physical cruelty Making repeated, violent, threatening gestures Assaulting with a weapon	Frightening with phone calls Challenging in public	Ostracizing Destroying personal property or clothing	Threatening total group exclusion	Arranging public humiliation Total group rejection / ostracizing

From the Teacher's Manual for Grades 2 and 3 for *No-Bullying Program: Preventing Bullying at School* by James Bitney and Beverly B. Title, Ph.D. Copyright © 2001 Hazelden Foundation, Center City, Minnesota. This page may be photocopied for training and implementation use only.

How to Use This Manual

This teacher's manual offers you material and detailed guidelines to lead second- and third-graders through seven 30- to 40-minute sessions of interactive learning. Factors that may change the amount of time each session takes are your personal teaching style and the number of activities you include.

Curriculum Goals

The goal for each of the seven sessions of the second- and third-grade curriculum follows:

- to introduce the *No-Bullying Program* to the children

- to help children define bullying, share ideas about bullying, and become more aware of the problems that result from bullying behaviors

- to help children identify and enumerate bullying behaviors

- to help children develop empathy for students who are bullied

- to help children learn how to respond to bullying behaviors

- to help children distinguish between tattling and telling, which is necessary for getting help with a bullying situation

- to help children learn the schoolwide consequences for engaging in bullying behaviors

Teaching Strategies

The *No-Bullying Program* incorporates a variety of teaching strategies to help you facilitate learning. These strategies include

- kinesthetic teaching tactics

- brainstorming

- drama and role playing

• group discussion

• student workbooks

• singing

Kinesthetic Teaching Tactics

An ancient Asian proverb states: "Tell me, I'll forget. Show me, I may remember. But involve me, and I'll understand." Kinesthetic teaching tactics *involve* the children and increase their ability to learn. With these techniques, learners get moving so that muscles may respond to the stimuli. Take every opportunity to allow the children to get on their feet, raise their hands, turn in their seats.

When the children aren't moving, make sure that you appeal to as many of their senses as possible. Capture their attention by using sight as well as sound. When children hear something and, at the same time, see the information written on the board or newsprint, they retain more of what's said. As you teach, then, frequently write out words and terms as you say them. If you've put a term or an idea on the board and then refer to it again, mark it with a circle, star, box, underscore, or checkmark each time you say it. Draw lines and arrows to connect words, and you'll establish connections between the terms in the students' minds. Consider using chalk or markers in a variety of colors to make the relationships between ideas or terms stand out visually even more.

Brainstorming

Brainstorming is an activity that supports the belief that "when we put our heads together to think, we're smarter than any one of us is when thinking alone." In a brainstorming session, all students are encouraged to speak quickly and briefly. A brainstorming activity is easy to conduct, and because every brainstorming response or idea is acceptable, almost all children are comfortable participating. Rather than getting responses from a small number of students, which frequently happens when the emphasis is put on asking for the "correct" answer, you draw out the perspective of many more students. As the children brainstorm, initial responses elicit new responses that pull together many ideas. This synergism tends to energize the children, making them eager to join in.

When the children brainstorm, list their responses (or words that capture them) on the board or newsprint. Don't comment upon the responses by saying things like "Good!" "Just what I was thinking," "I don't see how that fits, but I'll write it down anyway," or "Do you really mean that?" Your comments, positive or negative, can embarrass some children and can prevent others from saying anything at all. When brainstorming, be wary of searching for the "right" response and then stopping the activity when someone gives it. Instead, set a time limit for the brainstorming session and get as many responses as possible during that time, or end the activity when the children stop coming up with ideas.

Brainstorming helps children realize that they already know a great deal and that answers to questions they have may already lie within them. Thus, brainstorming helps the children value themselves and recognize that you value them.

Drama and Role Playing

In drama (skits) and role playing, children assume the identity of various characters. During role play, they may explore situations, identify problems, resolve conflicts, and create solutions. In other words, they deal with real-life matters in a safe situation. They can *safely* experience a range of emotions as they identify with characters in a challenging situation and work toward creative solutions.

Dr. Arnold P. Goldstein of Syracuse University, author of *Aggression Replacement Training: A Comprehensive Intervention for Aggressive Youth,* notes that role play is a very powerful learning strategy. For this reason, children should only be allowed to role-play behaviors that you want them to emulate; they should never act out negative behaviors in role plays. In the role plays during your classroom sessions, teachers or other adults should play roles that involve engaging in bullying behaviors.

Dramatizing a situation can provide insights for the children that simple discussion cannot. At the conclusion of a skit or role play, always offer participants the opportunity to express and process their feelings. Likewise, offer observers the chance to share their perceptions.

Group Discussion

A synergy occurs when children talk together and share ideas. In other words, the significance of their discussion is more than the sum of the individual responses and comments.

Student Workbooks

Each child needs a student workbook that contains pictures and activities to help students explore and remember the key concepts of the sessions.

Singing

At the close of each session in the *No-Bullying Program* curriculum for second and third grade, the children sing. The sessions end this way, first of all, because children love to sing. Singing adds a spirit of celebration, joy, and excitement to learning. At this age, children learn to sing by listening to and then repeating a song line by line (rote singing). Sing "No More Bullying" all the way through and then sing it phrase by phrase, having the children sing after you. The song is set to the melody of "Sailing, Sailing." You'll find the lyrics and the musical notation within each session.

Note: If you don't consider yourself a singer or are uncomfortable singing, ask someone to make an audiotape of the song that you can use with the children.

Understanding the Seven- to Eight-Year-Old Child

For the most part, the seven- to eight-year-old child exhibits the following characteristics. He or she

- trusts adults and older children

- needs and seeks adult encouragement and reassurance

- is dependent on parents for support, direction, approval, and love

- is very sensitive to both praise and criticism

- understands the concept of right and wrong but depends on adults to set standards for behavior

- is unsure of how he or she is behaving and asks questions like "Am I being good?"

- is interested in the work, concerns, and opinions of parents and other trusted adults

- learns by doing, therefore needs and enjoys hands-on learning activities and repetition

- has a clear gender identity and prefers to be with same-gender peers

- has a brief attention span and needs a variety of activities to stimulate interest

- requires a stable, consistent environment for learning

- possesses a rich dream and fantasy life, which he or she likes to explore as much as the real world

- is often moved by images and fantasies, but can be terrified by frightening or destructive images

- often behaves inconsistently

- possesses a sense of justice and fairness based on reciprocity ("If I behave in good ways, I will be rewarded. If I behave in bad ways, I will be punished.")

- is often unaware of the perspectives or feelings of others

- exhibits shyness around unfamiliar people

- can feel jealousy toward siblings and friends

- has occasional outbursts of temper and can behave inappropriately

- isn't always able to identify, own, and express feelings appropriately

Session Components

- **Goal** states the overall goal of the session.

- **Objectives** lists the learning outcomes of the session.

- **Materials** lists all the teaching devices necessary to present the session.

- **Preparing for the Session** contains instructions for the things you need to do before presenting the session.

- **Background for the Teacher** includes pertinent information

    — to help you set the educational content in context

    — to provide you with added information for professional growth

    — to give you the data you'll need to present the session most successfully

- **Session Plan** includes directions for presenting the session. Each session plan is composed of three parts: Beginning the Session, Leading the Session, and Concluding the Session.

    — *Beginning the Session* serves to gather and welcome the children, unite them as a group, review previous learning, and get them ready to work and share together.

    — *Leading the Session* provides clear, step-by-step instructions to help you guide the children through all the learning activities in the session, including group discussions, drama and role playing, brainstorming, and singing.

— *Concluding the Session* is much the same for every session and includes activities that serve to affirm the children in what they learned during the session and help them commit as individuals and as a school community to put an end to bullying.

- **Optional Activities** are included in some of the session plans and can be used to replace an activity in the plan, enhance the plan, or extend the session. Optional Activities may be used when you feel that the students need further work to master that lesson's objectives.

The session plans are formatted to give the children a total experience that is structured but hospitable, instructive but creative, and challenging but supportive. Each session is designed to build upon information in the previous sessions, so it's important to present all sessions in order. Because the format is consistent from session to session, the curriculum meets the needs of at-risk children for whom structure, stability, consistency, and enjoyment are critical. You can use the plans with confidence.

Session 1

Goal

To introduce the *No-Bullying Program* to the children.

Objectives

By the end of the session, the children will

- recognize and understand the No-Bullying logo
- begin to identify bullying behavior and its effects
- appreciate that their school is committed to putting an end to bullying

Materials

- No-Bullying poster
- lyrics of "No More Bullying" on newsprint (optional)
- newsprint and colored marker
- posterboard
- No-Bullying logo (from student workbook)
- scissors for each student
- crayons or colored markers
- glue sticks or paste
- safety pins
- cellophane tape

Preparing for the Session

Carefully read through the session plan. Make sure you have a No-Bullying poster, which you'll use during each of the classroom sessions.

Using the No-Bullying logo from the student workbook as a guide, trace the outline of the logo onto posterboard and then cut along the outline you've traced. This posterboard will serve as the backing for No-Bullying badges that the children will make during the session. Make a posterboard backing for each student. Bring enough safety pins to the session so that each child has one for his or her badge.

Note: If your school has laminating equipment, you might consider laminating the children's badges rather than using posterboard backing.

Review "No More Bullying," which is sung to the tune of "Sailing, Sailing" (see Leading the Session, step 6). The children will sing this song as you conclude each classroom session. Familiarize yourself with the sign for *no/not* in American Sign Language (ASL), which is illustrated in step 6, so you can teach the children how to use it as they sing the song. "No More Bullying" is in the student workbook, but if you want to display the lyrics for the students while they learn the song, print them on a piece of newsprint.

Background for the Teacher

It's important for teachers to understand that bullying isn't always obvious because children who bully often do so in concealed areas. At school, much of the time bullying occurs where adults aren't present, in places such as rest rooms, hallways, playground areas that are difficult to supervise, or empty classrooms. Simply because you don't witness bullying behaviors doesn't mean they aren't taking place. Teachers also need to understand that bullying *does* occur while adults are present, but we don't always recognize it as such because we've become desensitized to bullying. An important aspect of the *No-Bullying Program* is that it increases educators' ability to recognize and intervene on bullying behaviors that were previously overlooked entirely or viewed as unavoidable interactions among students.

Session Plan

Beginning the Session

Gather the children into a circle. Join the circle yourself. Introduce yourself and offer your own words of welcome. Then, beginning with the first child on your right, go around the circle and ask each child to introduce himself or herself and say one thing that makes him or her feel safe at school.

Leading the Session

1. Display the No-Bullying poster and read aloud the poster's message:

START CARING. STOP BULLYING!

   Ask the children what they think the poster means. Accept all replies, listing them on a sheet of newsprint.

2. Drawing on the children's ideas, lead a discussion about the poster with the group.

   • what types of things children who bully do

   • what happens to children who bully others

   • what happens to children who are being bullied

   • how bullying affects their school

   Again, list the children's ideas on newsprint. Save the newsprint sheet for use in step 4, and again for use in session 2.

3. After the discussion, tell the children that they will be talking more about bullying behavior—about students taking unfair advantage of others. Point out that your school wants to help stop all bullying in your school. Then say:

   "In our class time together, we will learn how to help each other and how and when to tell a trusted adult about bullying. However, whenever we talk about bullying *during this class,* we will never say the name of a child who is bullying others or a child who is being bullied. We will not talk about people; we'll only talk about bullying behaviors."

4. Drawing on the student's ideas from the discussion in step 2, help them express the following:

   • why they think children who bully do what they do

   • how they think a child who bullies might feel

   • how they think being bullied might make them feel

Add the children's ideas to the newsprint sheet. As the children talk about feelings, help them to avoid saying they'd feel "good" or "bad." Instead, encourage them to name feelings more specifically (for example, "sad," "angry," "frightened," "ashamed," and so on). If the children have difficulty in naming feelings, invite them to demonstrate the feeling through a facial expression or body language. If they are demonstrating anger, emphasize that they can show the feeling with their bodies, but they can't show it by hurting another student in any way. A list of feelings is included in the Appendix for your reference.

Tell the children that you'll save the newsprint sheet with their ideas for the next time they meet to talk about bullying. Say:

> "In our next session, we will identify bullying behavior, and
> we'll see if we need to make changes on this sheet."

5. Tell the children that they will each make a No-Bullying badge to wear. Distribute the scissors and the crayons or colored markers. Show the children where to turn in the student workbook to find the No-Bullying logo and ask them to cut it out. Let them color the logo in any fashion they wish. When the children are finished coloring, pass out the posterboard backings along with glue sticks or paste. (If you plan to laminate the logos, have the children write their names on the back, collect the logos, and have the children attach the pin after they are laminated.) Direct the children to affix their colored logos to the posterboard backing. Then have them tape a safety pin to the back of their badges. When the children finish, compliment them on their work. Tell the children they may put on the badges. Some students may need assistance with pinning on their badges, so be available to help. Encourage the children to wear their No-Bullying badges at school. Collect any materials from the badge-making project.

Tell the group that everyone in your school—children and adults—will be working hard at putting a stop to all bullying in school. Once again, assure the children that they will be learning ways to help one another, as well as learning how and when to tell a trusted adult about bullying.

6. Teach the children "No More Bullying," telling them that it's sung to the tune of "Sailing, Sailing," a song some of them will already know. If you have written the lyrics on a sheet of newsprint, display it for the children to see. Otherwise, you can have them turn to the song in their student workbooks.

No More Bullying

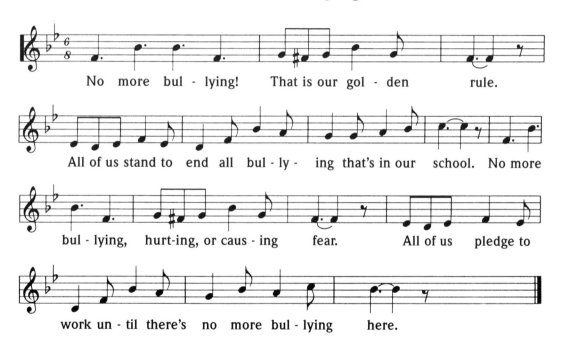

No more bul - lying! That is our gol - den rule.
All of us stand to end all bul - ly - ing that's in our school. No more
bul - lying, hurt-ing, or caus - ing fear. All of us pledge to
work un - til there's no more bul - lying here.

After the children know the words, teach them the ASL sign for *no/not* as illustrated below:

Tell the children that they can use the sign every time they sing the word *no*. Practice the song with the children, having them use the ASL sign.

Concluding the Session

Ask the children to form a circle around you. Instruct them to place their arms around one another's shoulders. Set the No-Bullying poster on the floor in the center of the circle. Join the circle yourself. Invite the children to sing "No More Bullying" while using the ASL *no/not* sign.

No More Bullying

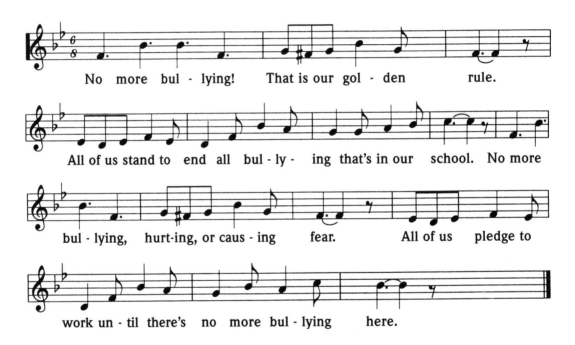

Ask the children to take one small step forward, thus tightening the circle, to show that they "stand together" in their commitment to put an end to bullying in their school. If you wish, conclude with handshakes or high fives all around.

Inform the children of when they'll have their next No-Bullying session. Tell them that when they meet, they will learn to identify bullying behavior.

Session 2

Goal

To help children define bullying, share ideas about bullying, and become more aware of the problems that result from bullying behaviors.

Objectives

By the end of the session, the children will

- know the definition of *bullying*

- share experiences of—and become more aware of—bullying behavior and its effects

- better understand that their school is committed to ending bullying

Materials

- No-Bullying poster

- chalkboard and chalk or newsprint and marker

- newsprint sheet with children's responses from session 1

- posterboard

- colored markers or art letters

- a pencil for each student

Preparing for the Session

Carefully read through the session plan. Using a marker or art letters and the posterboard, make a poster that reads:

BULLYING HAPPENS . . .

whenever someone uses his or her power

unfairly and *repeatedly* to hurt someone.

Note: You will need the Bullying Happens poster again during sessions 3 and 5, but many teachers find it useful to keep the poster in a visible spot and refer to it frequently while they deliver the remainder of the classroom curriculum.

Look over the What's Happening? survey in the Appendix so that you'll be ready to have the children fill it out. Make sure that the No-Bullying poster is prominently displayed in the meeting space.

Background for the Teacher

During this session, you will survey the children about bullying in your school using the What's Happening? survey located in the student workbook. You will also find it in the Appendix to this manual because your school's program director will probably require teachers to survey students at intervals following the delivery of the student curriculum. The schoolwide survey results will provide the program director with the information he or she needs to help school staff and students increase the effectiveness of the *No-Bullying Program.*

Session Plan

Beginning the Session

Gather the children into a circle. Draw attention to the No-Bullying poster. Invite volunteers to recall what the poster means. Remind the children:

"In our class time together, we will learn how to help each other and how and when to tell a trusted adult about bullying. However, whenever we talk about bullying *during this class,* we will never say the name of a child who is bullying others or a child who is being bullied. We will not talk about people; we'll only talk about bullying behaviors."

Leading the Session

1. To introduce this session, display the newsprint sheet listing the ideas about bullying that the children generated during session 1. Briefly review the information on the sheet, reminding the children of what they thought were

   • the types of things children who bully do

   • the consequences to children who bully others

   • the consequences to children who are being bullied

   • the effects of bullying on their school

2. Display the Bullying Happens poster you've prepared and read it aloud to the group.

BULLYING HAPPENS . . .

whenever someone uses his or her power

unfairly and *repeatedly* to hurt someone.

Then divide the chalkboard or a sheet of newsprint into three columns, labeling them as follows:

Physical Power   **Emotional Power**   **Social Power**

Explain these concepts to the students, giving examples of each. Tell the group that if someone uses the power he or she has in any of these three areas to hurt another person over and over, that person is engaging in bullying behaviors.

Once again, draw the children's attention to the newsprint sheet from session 1 that captured their initial ideas about bullying. For each of the responses they gave to the question "What types of things do children who bully do?" have the group determine what sort of power is unfairly used. List the children's responses under the appropriate heading. For example:

Physical Power	Emotional Power	Social Power
kicking	dirty looks	embarrassing
hitting	insults	keeping out of group
pushing	name-calling	gossiping
stealing	mean teasing	making fun of clothes
damaging belongings	holding nose	hurting friendships

Stress that bullying happens whenever someone *unfairly* uses power to hurt someone else *over and over* again.

3. Tell the children that now that they understand what counts as bullying, they will complete an important survey about bullying called What's Happening? Make sure the children understand that the survey isn't a test. Explain that the survey simply asks them to respond to statements about their lives at school. You will want to emphasize to the children that they shouldn't put their names on the survey; explain that its purpose is for the adults at school to learn more about what students *as a whole* experience at school, not to find out about any one student. Point out that there are no right or wrong answers and that some of the items may have more than one answer. Tell the children that they should mark as many answers for each statement as they feel are necessary to give their complete response.

4. Distribute pencils and show the students where to locate What's Happening? in the student workbook. Ask the children to complete it. If you feel that the children would be better served if you read the statements and possible responses aloud, go through the survey with the children.

5. When everyone is finished, help the children better "own" the survey by drawing attention to the fifth statement (*I think most of the bullying behavior*

that happens at our school happens . . .). Ask the children to raise their hands if they checked the first possible response *(in classrooms)*. Have one child record the number of student responses on the board or newsprint. Go through the five remaining locations doing the same. When they've considered each location, have the children count up the number of responses for each and determine where in the school they as a group believe most bullying behavior occurs.

6. Ask a different child to act as recorder. Repeat the procedure above for the tenth statement *(To help me feel safe at our school, I think adults should . . .)*.

When the children have finished discussing the last survey statement, assure them that you will convey their concerns about where bullying takes place in their school and what they'd like adults to do about it—as well as all other information from their survey—to other adults in the school, including the principal.

Collect the pencils and surveys.

Note: Have the students discuss their responses only to survey statements five and ten. All other survey statements contain information that needs to remain anonymous. However, you'll need to review all the surveys before you turn them over to the program director and prior to presenting the next session.

Concluding the Session

Ask the children to form a circle around you. Instruct them to place their arms around one another's shoulders. Set the No-Bullying poster on the floor in the center of the circle. Remind the children of the definition of bullying:

BULLYING HAPPENS . . .

whenever someone uses his or her power

unfairly and *repeatedly* to hurt someone.

Join the circle yourself and lead the children in singing "No More Bullying" while they use the ASL *no/not* sign.

No More Bullying

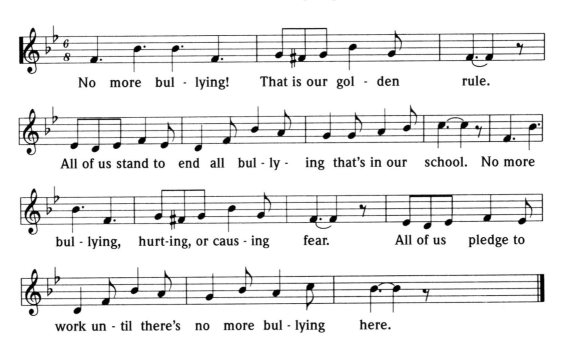

No more bul - lying! That is our gol - den rule.

All of us stand to end all bul - ly - ing that's in our school. No more

bul - lying, hurt-ing, or caus - ing fear. All of us pledge to

work un - til there's no more bul - lying here.

Encourage the children to use the ASL *no/not* sign anywhere or any-time they see bullying happening in their school.

Ask the children to take one small step forward, thus tightening the circle, to show that they "stand together" in their commitment to put an end to bullying in their school. If you wish, conclude with handshakes or high fives all around.

Inform the children of when they'll have their next No-Bullying session. Tell them that when they meet, they'll look at some examples of bullying behavior and how it affects others.

Session 3

Goal

To help children identify and enumerate bullying behaviors.

Objectives

By the end of the session, the children will

- create a list of bullying behaviors

- better understand how being bullied feels

Materials

- No-Bullying poster

- Bullying Happens poster

- Bullying Behavior Chart

- newsprint and colored markers

- "Bullying Denny"

- a pencil for each student

Preparing for the Session

Carefully read through the session plan, including "Bullying Denny," a skit about bullying behaviors, located in the Appendix. Arrange for two staff members or two parents, preferably one man and one woman, to play the roles of the children who bully when you present the skit during the session. Make three copies of "Bullying Denny," one for your own reference and the others for the adult actors.

Using a colored marker, divide a large sheet of newsprint into three columns. Start a Bullying Behaviors poster that the children will work on during the session; write in the title of the poster as well as the headings for the three columns:

BULLYING BEHAVIORS

Hurting someone's body or things	Hurting someone's feelings	Hurting someone's friendships

Make a copy of the Bullying Behavior Chart (page 8). Review the chart before the session and have it handy so you can refer to it as needed as you take the children through Leading the Session, step 6. Make sure the No-Bullying poster and the Bullying Happens poster are displayed prominently in the meeting space.

Background for the Teacher

Research shows that bullying behaviors include acts that harm people in the social or emotional arenas, as well as the physical.[1] No matter what form bullying takes, bullying behaviors are difficult for school staff to detect because they frequently occur out of our sight. As a teacher, you need to be aware that all types of bullying occur at school.

It's also important for you to keep in mind that bullying behaviors are *learned*. Consequently, school staff can help students who bully learn more appropriate ways of interacting when we consistently enforce consequences for engaging in bullying behaviors. Children who bully will come to see that bullying behaviors don't pay off. Because bullying behaviors are learned, we need to make sure that we don't unwittingly teach them to students. As previously mentioned, the research on aggression that Dr. Arnold P. Goldstein of Syracuse University has conducted

---

1. Dan Olweus, *Bullying at School: What We Know and What We Can Do* (Cambridge, Mass.: Blackwell Publishers, 1993), 9.

reveals the importance of not asking children to role-play behavior that we don't want them to emulate. For that reason, adults need to act out the bullying behaviors in "Bullying Denny."

Session Plan

Beginning the Session

Gather the children into a circle. Draw attention to the No-Bullying poster. Give the children the following reminder:

> "In our class time together, we will learn how to help each other and how and when to tell a trusted adult about bullying. However, whenever we talk about bullying *during this class,* we will never say the name of a child who is bullying others or a child who is being bullied. We will not talk about people; we'll only talk about bullying behaviors."

Then ask the children to recall the discussion during the previous session, in which they talked about the sorts of things children who bully do. Ask:

> "What types of things do children who bully do that makes their behavior different from that of other children?"

Look for responses that show the children understand that bullying includes the misuse of power and that the behaviors occur over and over.

Then have the group recall what they learned about bullying in their school from filling out What's Happening? Ask:

> "How does bullying affect our school?"

Leading the Session

1. Direct the children's attention to the Bullying Happens poster. Ask a volunteer to read it aloud.

> ## BULLYING HAPPENS . . .
> whenever someone uses his or her power
> *unfairly* and *repeatedly* to hurt someone.

2. Distribute the pencils and ask each student to turn to Why Kids Bully in the student workbook. Have a volunteer read aloud the statement "I think some kids bully other kids because . . ." Tell the children to think about the statement and then write at least two reasons why they think some kids bully others.

3. While the group is working, help the adult actors get ready to perform "Bullying Denny." Make sure that each adult has a copy of the skit and knows what you'd like him or her to do.

4. While the actors are preparing, invite the children to share what they wrote to finish the statement in their student workbooks. After each child who desires has had a chance to respond, tell the children they are now going to view a skit that will help them learn more about the behaviors of children who bully.

   Ask for a student volunteer to play the role of Denny, a child who is bullied at school. Tell "Denny" not to fight back or say anything mean to the other actors. Instead, the child playing Denny should *show* with his or her facial expressions and/or body language how he or she thinks Denny would feel.

5. Have the actors perform their skit for the group. Afterward, thank the participants.

   Lead the students in a discussion about the skit. Be aware that the presentation may have stirred up strong feelings that the children will need to talk about. Begin by asking the child who played Denny how it felt to be bullied. Then go on to ask the group the following questions:

   • If you were Denny, how would you feel?

   • Why would you feel that way?

   • Why would the other kids gang up on Denny?

   • Do you think it's okay for the other kids to say and do what they said and did to Denny?

   Be sure the children recognize how they'd feel if they were bullied.

6. Display the Bullying Behaviors poster.

BULLYING BEHAVIORS

| Hurting someone's body or things | Hurting someone's feelings | Hurting someone's friendships |

Invite the children to name and discuss the behaviors displayed by the actors who bullied Denny during the skit. List the children's responses under the appropriate columns on the poster. As the children offer their suggestions, refer to the Bullying Behavior Chart to suggest other behaviors that can be added to their list.

Draw the children's attention to the Bullying Happens poster. Tell the children that the behaviors they've listed are never nice ways to act and become bullying behaviors when the person who engages in them *uses his or her power unfairly and repeatedly.*

After you've finished the discussion, tell the children that you'll keep the Bullying Behaviors poster displayed in the meeting space and that they will continue to use this list (and add to it) to help them better recognize and deal with the problem of bullying in school.

Concluding the Session

Ask the children to form a circle around you. Instruct them to place their arms around one another's shoulders. Set the No-Bullying poster on the floor in the center of the circle. Join the circle yourself and lead the children in singing "No More Bullying" while they use the ASL *no/not* sign.

Encourage the children to use the ASL *no/not* sign anywhere or any-time they see bullying happening in their school.

No More Bullying

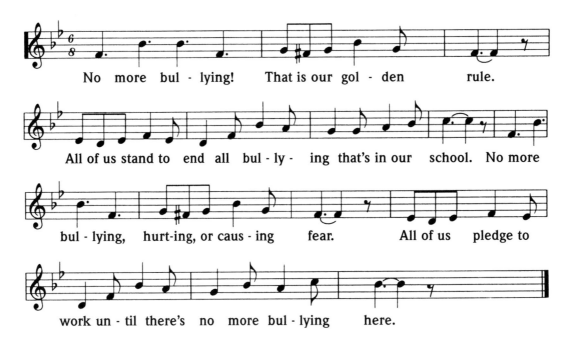

Ask the children to take one small step forward, thus tightening the circle, to show that they "stand together" in their commitment to put an end to bullying in their school. If you wish, conclude with handshakes or high fives all around.

Inform the children of when they'll have their next No-Bullying session. Tell them that when they meet, they'll learn a lot more about what happens to children who are bullied.

Optional Activities

If you want the children to have more practice identifying bullying behaviors, ask them to complete the Bullying Behaviors Word Search in the student workbook. An answer key for the word search is included in the Appendix.

Session 4

Goal

To help children develop empathy for students who are bullied.

Objectives

By the end of the session, the children will

- increase their level of empathy for children targeted by students who bully

Materials

- No-Bullying poster
- Bullying Behaviors poster
- Feelings List
- butcher paper
- crayons or colored markers
- cellophane tape
- pencils

Preparing for the Session

Carefully read through the session plan in advance. Review the diary entry in Leading the Session, step 3, so that you are ready to present it to the children. Also look over A Plan for Denny, located in the student workbook. Make a copy of the Feelings List from the Appendix so you can refer to it as necessary during the session. The children will be using the same Feelings List in their student workbooks. Using a long sheet of butcher paper, create a banner. In large letters, print "Bullying Makes Us Feel . . ." with a colored marker. Make sure you have enough wall space to hang the banner and a drawing by each student under the banner. Be sure that the No-Bullying poster and the Bullying Behaviors poster are displayed prominently in the room.

Background for the Teacher

No one deserves to be bullied. Bullying can only occur when a person takes unfair advantage of someone. Targeted children expend a great deal of energy to avoid being bullied. Nearly all their activity at school is focused on getting and staying safe. To put an end to bullying and to help targeted children, *all* the students need to learn to understand and empathize with them. Too often, however, such empathy is channeled into aggression toward the person who is exhibiting the bullying behavior. Unfortunately, this does little to end bullying. Children who bully are excited when the students they target fight back and when those who "take the side" of the targeted child display aggression. As you lead the children through this session, don't allow the children's empathy for a targeted student to turn to aggression toward the child who bullies. The goal isn't to avenge those who are bullied, but to help them feel protected and safe at school.

Session Plan

Beginning the Session

Gather the children into a circle. Give the children the following reminder:

> "In our class time together, we will learn how to help each other and how and when to tell a trusted adult about bullying. However, whenever we talk about bullying *during this class,* we will never say the name of a child who is bullying others or a child who is being bullied. We will not talk about people; we'll only talk about bullying behaviors."

Point out the No-Bullying poster, and then direct the students' attention to the Bullying Behaviors poster that they made during their last session. Ask if anyone has thought of behaviors he or she would like to add to it. Then remind the children that you will keep the poster displayed in the room, and they will continue to use it to help them deal with the problem of bullying in their school.

Leading the Session

1. Tell the children to turn to the Feelings List in their student workbooks. (Have your copy on hand for your reference.) Tell the children that they can use the names of the feelings on the list to help them describe how children their age might feel in a variety of situations. Ask the children the questions listed below, each of which begins with "How might someone your age feel if he or she . . ."

   • just made the winning score in a game?

   • ate a whole box of chocolate candy?

   • lost a favorite toy?

   • won a prize?

   • had an argument with a best friend?

   • got called on in class and didn't know the answer?

   Go on to ask "What types of things might make someone your age feel . . ."

   • happy?

   • sad?

   • lonely?

   • nervous?

   • afraid?

2. Invite the children to recall the skit about Denny from the last session. Ask volunteers to explain what happened to Denny. Encourage the children to find the words from the Feelings List that tell how they think Denny felt. Tell them they can also show the feeling with a facial expression or body language. Emphasize that they must not show any feeling in a way that hurts others.

3. Have the children quiet themselves inside and outside to hear a story. Explain that the story comes from a diary written by someone who is the same age as they are, and then read the following entry to the children:

Dear Diary,

I hate school! I wish I didn't have to go. Some of the kids there are always picking on me. They're mean. They follow me around the playground. They make fun of me. They always say they're going to beat me up. It's not fair! I'm scared all the time.

One day, this really big kid pushed me down and took my lunch. I didn't know what to do, so I just went hungry. Last week, this girl colored all over a picture I drew. I handed it in, but it was a mess. The teacher told me that I was not a good worker. See, even the teacher doesn't like me.

I want to punch those kids who are bullying me and tell them to leave me alone or go away, but I just can't. I get this real sick feeling in my stomach. It makes me want to cry, but I know that would just make them laugh.

Even the kids who used to be my friends aren't nice anymore. Maybe they're afraid of getting hurt, too. Or maybe they just don't like me anymore. I don't know. What I do know is that I wish some big giant would come in the middle of the night and squish the school. Then I wouldn't have to go there.

What do you think, Diary? What should I do? Do you have a plan? I don't.

Your friend,

Denny

4. Invite the children to share their initial reactions to the story. Ask them if they were surprised at the end when they discovered that this was from *Denny's* diary. Then draw attention to the Feelings List and ask:

- How does Denny feel?

- Do you think Denny has a right to feel the way he does?

- How do you feel when you see someone else being bullied?

5. Distribute the crayons or colored markers. Divide the children into two groups and ask them to turn to Bullying Makes Us Feel in the student workbook. Ask the children in the first group to draw a picture that shows how someone their age might feel if *he* or *she* were being bullied. Instruct the children in the second group to draw a picture that shows how someone their age might feel if he or she saw *someone else* being bullied. Tell the children to circle the sentence on the page that describes which picture they are drawing.

While the children draw, hang the Bullying Makes Us Feel banner. When the children are finished drawing, call on members of the first group to explain their drawings to the class. Invite the first group to tape their drawings under the banner. Then ask members of the second group to explain their drawings to the class. Invite the second group to tape their drawings under the banner. Point out that bullying never makes people feel happy.

6. Read aloud to the children the last paragraph of the diary entry again: *"What do you think, Diary? What should I do? Do you have a plan? I don't."*

Then ask:

> "What could you do if you were being bullied or you saw someone else being bullied?"

Accept all replies but gently discourage any suggestions of retaliation. Tell the children that they may feel like hurting someone back, but encourage them to think about how that would make things worse in the long run.

Distribute pencils to the students. Ask them to turn to A Plan for Denny in the student workbook. Go through the steps outlined on the sheet with the children. Point out that no one deserves to be bullied, but that bullying back isn't an option. Stress the importance of telling a caring adult about the bullying. Collect the crayons or colored markers and pencils.

Concluding the Session

Ask the children to form a circle around you. Instruct them to place their arms around one another's shoulders. Set the No-Bullying poster on the floor in the center of the circle. Join the circle yourself and lead the children in singing "No More Bullying" while they use the ASL *no/not* sign.

No More Bullying

No more bul - lying! That is our gol - den rule.

All of us stand to end all bul - ly - ing that's in our school. No more

bul - lying, hurt-ing, or caus - ing fear. All of us pledge to

work un - til there's no more bul - lying here.

Encourage the children to use the ASL *no/not* sign anywhere or anytime they see bullying happening in their school.

Ask the children to take one small step forward, thus tightening the circle, to show that they "stand together" in their commitment to put an end to bullying in their school. If you wish, conclude with handshakes or high fives all around.

Inform the children of when they'll have their next No-Bullying session. Tell them that when they meet, they'll learn some important things they can do when they or someone else is being bullied.

Session 5

Goal

To help children learn how to respond to bullying behaviors.

Objectives

By the end of the session, the children will

- become aware of the need to respond immediately to bullying behavior
- develop skills to respond to bullying behavior
- be able to use assertive posture and tone of voice

Materials

- No-Bullying poster
- Bullying Happens poster
- Bullying Behaviors poster
- Bullying Behavior Chart
- A Plan for Denny
- newsprint and colored markers
- list pairing students
- crayons or colored markers
- scissors for each student

Preparing for the Session

Carefully read through the session plan, paying special attention to the Power Tools described in Background for the Teacher. On a separate piece of newsprint, print the name of each of the four Power Tools you'll be talking about in this session: Word Power, Find a Friend, Run Away, and School Rule. Print the following I-statement formula on a separate sheet of newsprint:

> "I don't like it when you _____ ,
>
> and I want you to stop."

Make a School Rule formula, reading:

> "Our school has a rule against bullying, and
>
> _____ is breaking the rule."
> (identify bullying behavior)

Think about the students in your classroom. You know some students to be temperamentally meek, while others are more aggressive. Create a list for the activity in Leading the Session, step 9, pairing students who tend to be submissive with students for whom assertive behavior is likely to come more naturally.

Make sure the No-Bullying poster, the Bullying Happens poster, and the Bullying Behaviors poster are prominently displayed in the meeting space.

Background for the Teacher

As mentioned in the Introduction, researchers Debra Pepler and Wendy Craig at York University in Toronto, Canada, emphasize the importance of the targeted child's response to the first encounter with a student who bullies. When one student first attempts to bully another, the aggressive student doesn't yet have much power over the targeted student; however, if the early bullying behavior succeeds, the bullying will continue and likely become more severe. The power of the student who bullies can increase with each episode.

Bullying behavior catches many targeted children off-guard. Because an immediate response to any bullying episode is critical, it's important for children to know appropriate responses and to have practiced them so they can act effectively when they are under the stress of an actual bullying situation.

In the *No-Bullying Program* curriculum for kindergarten and first grade, the children learned three strategies for responding to bullying: Word Power, Find a Friend, and Run Away. We call these strategies Power Tools because we want children who are bullied to know that they, too, have power—power to fix things, which is what you do with tools. You will review those tools in this session and then introduce a fourth Power Tool, School Rule, to your students. (If this is the first year that your school is implementing the *No-Bullying Program,* you will be introducing all four of the tools to your students. If this is the case, you might want to cover the material in two sessions rather than one. Please refer to the teacher's manual for kindergarten and first grade to see the activities used for teaching Word Power, Find a Friend, and Run Away.) The *No-Bullying Program* curriculum for each successive grade-range level will review the tools taught in the earlier grades and add more responses to the students' repertoire, or toolbox. The purpose of adding Power Tools each year isn't to replace the tools learned at the lower grades, but to provide the students with a wider range of possible responses. The complete set of Power Tools (kindergarten through eighth grade) is included in the Appendix so you'll know what students in the higher grades are learning. The tools learned in kindergarten and first grade are the following:

Word Power

Steps in Word Power: Make eye contact with the student who is bullying and use an I-statement while making the ASL *no/not* sign.

EXAMPLE OF WORD POWER:

STUDENT WHO BULLIES: "You are so stupid. The way you play video games is dumb."

TARGETED STUDENT: "I don't like it when you call me names, and I want you to stop."

Find a Friend

Steps in Find a Friend: Call out to nearby students, say you're being bullied, and ask them to come stand with you and make the ASL *no/not* sign.

EXAMPLE OF FIND A FRIEND:

STUDENT WHO BULLIES: "Hey, stupid, I want that ball. Give it to me if you know what's good for you."

TARGETED STUDENT: "Tyler, Melissa, Mark, I'm getting hassled. Help me out. Stand here with me and make the sign."

Run Away

Steps in Run Away: Choose a safe direction, run, and tell an adult as soon as you can.

EXAMPLE OF RUN AWAY:

STUDENT WHO BULLIES: "I'm going to wipe you off the face of the earth."

TARGETED STUDENT: Looks to see if the playground supervisor is anywhere in sight, sees her, and runs across the playground to her.

The tool that is added for second and third grade is

School Rule

Steps in School Rule: Use an assertive (sure) posture and tone of voice while delivering the School Rule formula: "Our school has a rule against bullying, and _____ is breaking the rule."
        (identify bullying behavior)

EXAMPLE OF SCHOOL RULE:

STUDENT WHO BULLIES: "Hey, get out of my way, punk. I need to get my lunch."

TARGETED STUDENT: Using an assertive posture and tone of voice, says, "Our school has a rule against bullying, and cutting in line and name-calling are breaking the rule."

Word Power is a simplified I-statement. You'll notice that it doesn't include the feelings information that a typical I-statement does. Following the advice of William Voors, author of *The Parent's Book about Bullying: Changing the Course of Your Child's Life* (see Resources), we've eliminated that portion of the statement.[1] Asking young children to identify specific feelings would increase the difficulty they have in delivering an assertive response when under pressure in a bullying situation. In addition, students who bully enjoy influencing the emotional affect of those they target, and telling the feeling may just confirm that his or her behavior is having its intended effect.

Find a Friend and Run Away are easier concepts and will take less time to review than Word Power. Run Away is a straightforward tool, but make sure you emphasize that the targeted child choose a safe direction in which to run. There have been cases where targeted children have run into the path of a car or toward other dangers. Tell the children that it is best to run toward adults or other children who will help.

When reviewing these tools, also review how the children decide what tool to use in a specific bullying incident. The best indicator students can use is to listen to their feelings. If they feel afraid, the best choices would be Run Away or Find a Friend. Although, as educators we want to encourage students to be assertive, if a student has bullied another child more than once or twice, and thus established a power imbalance, an I-statement will not be an effective tool.

School Rule is also a pretty straightforward tool, but to be effective, the child must deliver the statement assertively. Much of your focus in teaching this tool is to convey what an assertive attitude *looks* like. For the temperamentally meek child and for the more aggressive child, becoming comfortable with the middle ground of assertiveness will be challenging. When they are paired with children who naturally tend to be assertive for the assertive attitude exercise in Leading the Session, step 9, the children on the ends of the continuum will get a chance to see peers model effective behavior.

If you feel that reviewing the three Power Tools and teaching School Rule is too much to accomplish in one session, you may do the review during the session, and then follow up as soon as possible, ideally the next day, with the new tool.

---

1. William Voors, *The Parent's Book about Bullying: Changing the Course of Your Child's Life* (Center City, Minn.: Hazelden, 2000), 71–72.

Session Plan

Beginning the Session

Gather the children into a circle. Give the children this reminder:

> "In our class time together, we will learn how to help each other and how and when to tell a trusted adult about bullying. However, whenever we talk about bullying *during this class,* we will never say the name of a child who is bullying others or a child who is being bullied. We will not talk about people; we'll only talk about bullying behaviors."

Invite the children to recall the skit about Denny being bullied at school. Then ask the students if they remember the plan for Denny that they talked about during the previous session. Fill in missing information if they have trouble recalling the following four steps:

Step 1: Name the Problem

Step 2: Know the Feelings

Step 3: Ask for Help

Step 4: Help Yourself

Stress that Help Yourself doesn't mean that the students should ever bully back. Remind them that telling an adult is often necessary to stop a child who bullies from hurting you or someone else. But tell them that today they'll be learning some useful things they can do to help themselves or others who are being bullied.

Leading the Session

1. Point to the Bullying Happens poster and take a moment to review the definition:

BULLYING HAPPENS . . .

whenever someone uses his or her power

unfairly and *repeatedly* to hurt someone.

---

2. Tell the children it's important that they know what to do in case someone should try to bully them. Say that in this session they will review the three Power Tools they learned in kindergarten and first grade. Recall that Power Tools are the things they can do when they are being bullied. Remind them that we call these Power Tools because they will help the children learn good ways to use their power in difficult situations.

3. Display the newsprint on which you've printed "Word Power" and ask the children what they remember about this tool. You might need to remind the children that Word Power is an easy way to tell someone that you don't like the way they're behaving toward you or someone else. Display the newsprint on which you've printed the I-statement formula. Give the children an example of a simplified I-statement, filling in the blank. For example: "I don't like it when you take my crayons without asking, and I want you to stop." Ask the children to call out other examples. Ask if they have used the tool and what happened when they did. (Again, remind the children not to say the name of any child who has bullied or has been bullied.)

4. After the children have a good idea of what an I-statement sounds like, ask them to choose a partner so they can practice making I-statements. Tell the children that one partner can choose a behavior from the Bullying Behaviors poster and ask the other child to respond with an I-statement. Explain that it's very important that they don't act out any bullying behavior, but that they must only say it to their partner. Ask the children to take turns choosing the behavior or responding with an I-statement.

5. Gather the children into a circle again. Explain that I-statements are often a good way to respond when someone behaves in a way that hurts you or someone else. But as with real tools, you can't use the same one for every job. If a student has bullied you more than once or twice, I-statements probably won't work. Or, if this is the first time a student picks on you but you feel afraid, an I-statement probably won't work.

Remind them that, for this reason, in kindergarten and first grade they learned three Power Tools for dealing with students who bully. Ask if anyone remembers what the other two tools are. After the children have had a chance to respond, display the newsprint sheets on which you printed "Find a Friend" and "Run Away." Ask if the students have used either of these tools and what happened. Explain that these are good tools to use when someone has bullied another student more than once or twice. They are even good tools to use the first time another student picks on you if you feel afraid to use Word Power. Review the steps in Find a Friend: call out to nearby students, say you're being bullied, and ask them to come stand with you and make the ASL *no/not* sign. For example: "Tyler, Melissa, Mark, I'm getting hassled. Help me out. Stand here with me and make the sign." Have the children role-play Find a Friend. Stress that no one is to act out the part of the child who bullies. After the children have finished role playing Find a Friend, go over the steps of Run Away: choose a safe direction, run, and tell an adult as soon as you can.

6. Tell the children that today they will learn another tool to add to their toolboxes. Display the newsprint sheet on which you printed "School Rule." Tell the children that your school has a rule against bullying and that a student who uses *any* bullying behavior is breaking the rule. Help the students learn the difference between bullying and nonbullying behaviors by doing the first Power Tools exercise in the student workbook.

Ask a volunteer to read one bullying behavior from the Bullying Behaviors poster. Then demonstrate School Rule, filling in the blank of the School Rule formula with the behavior the volunteer called out. Stand and speak assertively as you say:

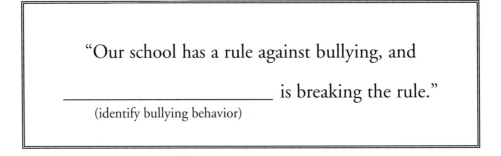

"Our school has a rule against bullying, and

_____ is breaking the rule."
  (identify bullying behavior)

7. Tell the children to think about real power tools that they've seen adults use. Ask what the adult did first to get the power tool to work. Look for or supply the response that before a power tool will work, it has to be plugged in. Tell the children that power tools that run on electricity are for adults only. The Power Tools children can use to fix situations with children who bully run on assertiveness, or making their bodies look *sure* and making their voices sound *sure*. Tell the children that when they want to use School Rule, they plug in by the way they're standing and their tone of voice.

Demonstrate submissive (soft), aggressive (mean), and assertive (sure) stances and voices. (**Note:** Children this age might not understand the words *submissive, aggressive,* and *assertive.* Age-appropriate options are given in parentheses.) Mix and match them. For instance, demonstrate an assertive tone of voice with an assertive stance. Then demonstrate an assertive tone of voice with a submissive stance. Go through a variety of combinations until the children see that to deliver School Rule effectively, they must both stand *and* speak assertively.

8. Ask the children to form a circle and practice plugging in. Watch as the children stand assertively and use an assertive tone of voice to say the first part of the School Rule formula: "Our school has a rule against bullying . . ." Look for students who are doing a good job with assertiveness and ask them to demonstrate the stance and tone of voice for the other children.

9. Review with the students the poster on which you've printed the School Rule formula:

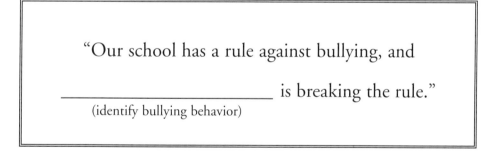

"Our school has a rule against bullying, and

_____ is breaking the rule."
    (identify bullying behavior)

Inform the children that when they need to use School Rule in a real bullying situation, they are to fill in the blank by naming the bullying behavior they have observed. Tell them that now you want them to practice School Rule with a partner that you'll announce. When they are practicing, they are to fill in the blank with the bullying behavior their partner chooses to read from the Bullying Behaviors poster. Emphasize that no one is allowed to act out bullying behavior. Read off the partners from the list you've prepared. Then carefully watch those children who may have the most trouble being assertive and give assistance as needed. When you feel the children have had enough practice, instruct them to sit down.

10. Ask the children to look at the newsprint sheets with the names of the other three Power Tools. Ask if they think some of these tools might work better if they were also "plugged in." Tell them that knowing how to plug in their tools will make these tools more powerful. (**Note:** If, earlier in the session, students said they had used some of the Power Tools without much success, you might suggest that they now will have more power behind these tools.)

11. To reinforce the children's perception that they always have these Power Tools available to them when they are being bullied, ask them to turn to the page with the Power Tools in their student workbooks. Distribute the crayons or colored markers and the scissors. Have the children color the four Power Tools and cut them out. Have them find the page with the pictures of three children. The students are to color and cut out the child who looks "plugged in"—in other words, they are to select the assertive child. Ask the children to fold and tape My Toolbox, found in the student workbook, and put their tools and "plugged-in" student inside so they'll always have them ready.

12. Tell the children that everyone has power, and they have learned some ways to use their power to help keep themselves and others safe. Remind them that it is very important to use their power to be helpful, not hurtful. Collect the crayons or colored markers.

Concluding the Session

Ask the children to form a circle around you. Instruct them to place their arms around one another's shoulders. Set the No-Bullying poster on the floor in the center of the circle. Join the circle yourself and lead the children in singing "No More Bullying" while they use the ASL *no/not* sign.

Encourage the children to use the ASL *no/not* sign anywhere or anytime they see bullying happening in their school.

No More Bullying

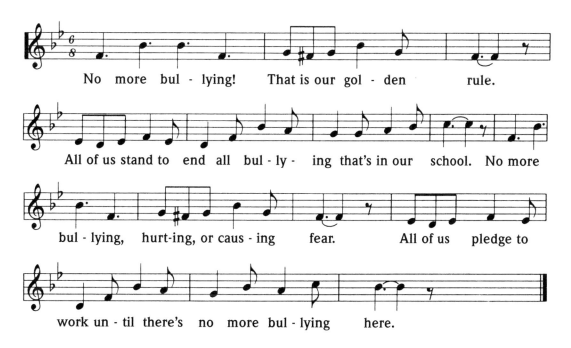

No more bul - lying! That is our gol - den rule.

All of us stand to end all bul - ly - ing that's in our school. No more

bul - lying, hurt-ing, or caus - ing fear. All of us pledge to

work un - til there's no more bul - lying here.

Ask the children to take one small step forward, thus tightening the circle, to show that they "stand together" in their commitment to put an end to bullying in their school. If you wish, conclude with handshakes or high fives all around.

Inform the children of when they'll have their next No-Bullying session. Tell them that when they meet, they'll learn some very important information about how to tell an adult about bullying so they can get help.

Session 6

Goal

To help children distinguish between tattling and telling, which is necessary for getting help with a bullying situation.

Objectives

By the end of the session, the children will

- know the definitions of *tattling* and *telling*

- understand the difference between tattling and telling

- recognize that to get help with bullying, they need to tell someone they trust

- appreciate how adults in their school are willing to help stop bullying

- learn their school's procedure for reporting bullying behavior

Materials

- No-Bullying poster

- Bullying Behaviors poster

- chalkboard and chalk or newsprint and marker

- posterboard

- colored markers or art letters

- a pencil for each student

Preparing for the Session

Carefully read through the entire session plan. On posterboard, use a colored marker or art letters to make a poster that reads:

> **TATTLING** is talking to someone about a problem just to get someone else in trouble, to get my own way, or to make myself look good.

On a second sheet of posterboard, make a poster that reads:

> **TELLING** is talking to someone I trust about a problem because I may be or someone else may be getting hurt.

Read Tattling or Telling? located in the student workbook. Review the procedure your school has established for reporting bullying behavior. If you have any questions about the procedure, talk with the program director before presenting the session to the children. Be prepared to explain to the children all of the specific information they'll need for reporting, including *how* they are to report, to *whom* they are to report, and *when* and *where* they are to report.

Carefully consider using the two optional activities, which are found after Concluding the Session. If you decide to use one or both, make all of the necessary arrangements. Make sure the No-Bullying poster and the Bullying Behaviors poster are prominently displayed in the meeting space.

Background for the Teacher

Second- and third-graders are beginning to develop a sense of allegiance to the peer group, which will grow stronger as students approach adolescence. But this is not to say that normal seven- and eight-year-olds don't tattle on one another. However, they generally do so to get their own way or to look "better" in the eyes of adults. Your challenge in presenting this session is to discourage tattling while helping the children recognize that it is appropriate to tell when they are being bullied or when they witness bullying. An open and nonjudgmental attitude on your part will go a long way in helping children tell and not tattle.

As you present the session, remember that targeted children and those who witness bullying are afraid to tell about bullying behavior. They fear both physical retribution and social ostracism. Make sure the students understand that you and all school staff are committed to protecting students from bullying. Tell them that the adults at the school will keep an eye on any child who is reported for engaging in bullying behavior and that the child will be held responsible for any further bullying.

Session Plan

Beginning the Session

Gather the children into a circle. Draw attention to the No-Bullying poster. Invite the children to recall the four Power Tools they talked about during their last session. Then ask them if they think that they can always take care of a bullying situation themselves. Listen to their responses. Assure them that adults at school don't expect them to put an end to bullying at school without help from adults. Then ask the students what they think would be the best thing to do if

- they were being bullied

- they saw someone else being bullied

Tell the children that in this session they will learn how to *tell* about bullying and get help without feeling that they're *tattling*. Give the children this reminder:

> "In our class time together, we will learn how to help each other and how and when to tell a trusted adult about bullying. However, whenever we talk about bullying *during this class,* we will never say the name of a child who is bullying others or a child who is being bullied. We will not talk about people; we'll only talk about bullying behaviors."

Leading the Session

1. Write the word *tattling* on the chalkboard or newsprint. Ask the children to brainstorm what they think tattling is. Record all ideas on the board or newsprint. Drawing on the children's ideas, help them recognize that tattling is talking to someone about a problem

   • just to get someone else in trouble

   • just to get their own way

   • just to make themselves look good and someone else look bad

   Tell the children when we do these things, we're tattling.

2. Display the Tattling poster you've made. Read the definition aloud to the group:

   TATTLING is talking to someone about a problem just to get someone else in trouble, to get my own way, or to make myself look good.

   Invite the children to offer examples of tattling, but emphasize that they should just talk about situations and not say the names of other children. If the children confuse tattling with telling, gently correct the misunderstanding.

3. Write the word *telling* on the board or newsprint. Ask the children to brainstorm what they think telling is. Record all ideas on the board or newsprint.

   Drawing on the children's ideas, help them recognize that telling is speaking to an adult about a problem to get help for oneself or another person.

   Display the Telling poster you've made. Read the definition aloud to the group:

> **TELLING** is talking to someone I trust
> about a problem because I may be
> or someone else may be getting hurt.

Invite the children to offer examples of telling, emphasizing that *during this class* they should talk only about situations and not say the names of other children. Again, should the children confuse telling with tattling, gently correct the misunderstanding.

5. Distribute the pencils and ask the children to turn to Tattling or Telling? in their student workbooks. Depending on the reading level of the children, you may ask volunteers to read aloud each of the four stories, or you may read the stories aloud and have the students follow along. At the end of each story, read the follow-up question and have the children circle whether they think the child in the story was tattling or telling. After you have completed all four stories, return to each and ask for a show of hands to determine how many children circled tattling and how many circled telling for each story. (**Note:** The correct responses are—Lisa = tattling; Luiz = telling; Shanna = telling; Jamhal = tattling.)

6. Take time to discuss the difference between tattling and telling. In the discussion, help the children understand that tattling gets someone *into* trouble, while telling helps get someone *out* of trouble. Emphasize to the children that when they are being bullied and their bodies, feelings, or things are being hurt, or when they see someone else being bullied and hurt in those ways, they need to tell a trusted adult in their school.

Outline for the children the procedure your school has agreed upon for reporting bullying. Tell them *how* they are to report, to *whom* they are to report, *when* and *where* they are to report, and any other information they need to know. Make sure the children understand that when they tell about bullying, their anonymity will be ensured and that an adult *will* step in to help and protect. Collect the pencils.

Concluding the Session

Ask the children to form a circle around you. Instruct them to place their arms around one another's shoulders. Set the No-Bullying poster on the floor in the center of the circle. Join the circle yourself and lead the children in singing "No More Bullying" while they use the ASL *no/not* sign.

No More Bullying

No more bul-lying! That is our gol-den rule. All of us stand to end all bul-ly-ing that's in our school. No more bul-lying, hurt-ing, or caus-ing fear. All of us pledge to work un-til there's no more bul-lying here.

Encourage the children to continue to use the ASL *no/not* sign anywhere or anytime they see bullying happening in their school.

Ask the children to take one small step forward, thus tightening the circle, to show that they "stand together" in their commitment to put an end to bullying in their school. If you wish, conclude with handshakes or high fives all around.

Inform the children of when they'll have their next No-Bullying session. Tell them that when they meet, the principal will join them to explain what will happen to children who engage in bullying behaviors.

Optional Activities

1. To enhance the session, divide the class into small groups. Have them role-play how to tell an adult about bullying. This practice will give children the confidence to approach adults for aid. It will also help them better distinguish between tattling and telling.

   You may want to invite older students (from the fourth and/or fifth grades), peer counselors, or conflict mediators to present a few role plays to the children in your class so your students can see appropriate examples of telling to get someone out of trouble.

2. To enhance Leading the Session, step 6, create a Bullying Report Card that will remind students of your school's procedure for reporting bullying behavior. Simply outline the procedure, duplicate it on construction paper or index cards, and give the cards to the children so they can tape them in their student workbooks or keep them with them.

Session 7

Goal

To help children learn the schoolwide consequences for engaging in bullying behaviors.

Objectives

By the end of the session, the children will

- understand the meaning of *consequences*
- know the schoolwide consequences for engaging in bullying behavior
- better understand that all adults in the school are committed to making the school a safe and secure place

Materials

- No-Bullying poster
- Bullying Behaviors poster
- chalkboard and chalk or newsprint and marker
- posterboard or newsprint and colored markers
- crayons or colored markers

Preparing for the Session

Carefully read through the entire session plan. On the posterboard, make a large poster called "Bullying Consequences." Simplifying the language of the official school policy into words the children will understand, list the consequences the school has established for engaging in bullying behaviors.

Make arrangements to have the principal present the core of the session. Consider whether you want to use the optional activity located after Concluding the Session. If you choose to issue Bullying Consequences cards to the students, you'll need to put the information that's on the Bullying Consequences poster onto index cards or construction paper so you can pass them out to the students. Make sure that the No-Bullying poster and the Bullying Behaviors poster are prominently displayed in the meeting space.

Background for the Teacher

Even the youngest children can understand the concept of consequences. Unfortunately, many students have experienced that consequences aren't always fairly applied. They need powerful reassurance that your school has no tolerance whatsoever for bullying behavior and that the staff at your school will impose swift and strict consequences when it does occur. Obtaining and maintaining the children's trust is critical to the success of the *No-Bullying Program*. The children need to trust that responsible and caring adults will intervene when a child engages in bullying behavior and that the adults will keep them safe.

Session Plan

Beginning the Session

Gather the children into a circle. Include the school principal in the circle, reminding the children that he or she will be a visitor to their class today. Draw attention to the No-Bullying poster. Ask the children to explain its purpose. Then invite the children to recall the difference between tattling and telling. Ask:

- What gets someone *into* trouble, tattling or telling?
  (Tattling.)

- What gets someone *out* of trouble, tattling or telling?
  (Telling.)

Take time to correct any misunderstandings. Give the children this reminder:

> "In our class time together, we will learn how to help each other and how and when to tell a trusted adult about bullying. However, whenever we talk about bullying *during this class*, we will never say the name of a child who is bullying others or a child who is being bullied. We will not talk about people; we'll only talk about bullying behaviors."

Ask the children to look over the Bullying Behaviors poster and ask whether they want you to add to it any behavior they may have noticed is missing.

Leading the Session

1. Print the word *consequences* on the board or newsprint. Read the word aloud and ask if anyone knows what it means. Record student responses on the board or newsprint.

2. Drawing on the children's ideas, help them devise a definition of consequences. If they need prompting, you can say:

> "After we say or do something, a consequence is *what might happen next.*"

Use the following questions to help them understand the concept of consequences:

- If you put your hand in very hot water, what might happen next?

- If you win a race, what might happen next?

- If you eat too much at supper, what might happen next?

- If you don't do your homework, what might happen next?

- If you bully someone at school, what might happen next?

Tell the children that their principal will talk to them about the consequences—about what will happen next—to students who bully others in their school.

3. The school principal will now talk to the children about your school's no-tolerance rule for bullying behavior and explain the consequences for engaging in bullying. Make sure the principal has access to and discusses the Bullying Consequences poster you made for the session. The principal should also take time to reassure the children that school staff will support and protect students who are bullied.

4. When the principal completes his or her presentation, ask the children where they'd like to display the Bullying Consequences poster in their classroom. Help the children hang the poster.

5. Briefly go through the items on the poster. Let the children know that you—and all the other adults in the school—agree with the consequences, promise to be supportive of students who want to put an end to bullying behaviors in their school and who tell about bullying, and pledge to protect all students who are bullied.

6. Help the children locate What Might Happen Next? in their student workbooks. Ask them to think about the consequences for bullying that the principal explained. Have them draw a picture of one thing that might happen next if someone at school engages in bullying behavior.

Concluding the Session

Invite the principal to join the children as they form a circle around you. Instruct them to place their arms around one another's shoulders. Set the No-Bullying poster on the floor in the center of the circle. Join the circle yourself and lead the children in singing "No More Bullying" while they use the ASL *no/not* sign.

Encourage the children to use the ASL *no/not* sign anywhere or anytime they see bullying happening in their school.

No More Bullying

No more bul - lying! That is our gol - den rule.

All of us stand to end all bul - ly - ing that's in our school. No more

bul - lying, hurt-ing, or caus - ing fear. All of us pledge to

work un - til there's no more bul - lying here.

Ask the children to take one small step forward, thus tightening the circle, to show that they "stand together" in their commitment to put an end to bullying in their school. Tell the students that now each of them can sign his or her name on the No-Bullying poster to show that all students will work together with adults at school to put an end to bullying. Then ask the principal to add his or her signature before signing the poster yourself.

If you wish, conclude with handshakes or high fives all around. Thank the children for all their good work and their willingness to put an end to bullying in their school.

Optional Activities

To help the students remember the consequences for engaging in bullying behavior, put the information on the Bullying Consequences poster onto index cards or construction paper. Give each student a copy, which they can keep with them.

Appendix

Feelings List

afraid	excited	loved
aggressive	frightened	miserable
amused	frustrated	nervous
angry	furious	powerful
anxious	glad	powerless
appreciated	guilty	proud
bitter	happy	rejected
bored	hopeful	relieved
concerned	hopeless	sad
confused	hurt	safe
contented	insecure	tense
disappointed	inspired	unloved
discouraged	jealous	wanted
enthusiastic	joyful	worthless
envious	lonely	worthwhile

What's Happening?

1. I am a

   ☐ Girl   ☐ Boy

2. I get bullied at school.
   I am pushed, kicked, or hit.

   ☐ Never   ☐ Once in a while

   ☐ A lot   ☐ Every day

3. I get bullied at school. I am called names,
   put down, teased, or left out of a group.

   ☐ Never   ☐ Once in a while

   ☐ A lot   ☐ Every day

4. I bully others at school.

   ☐ Never   ☐ Once in a while

   ☐ A lot   ☐ Every day

5. I think most of the bullying behavior
   that happens at our school happens

   ☐ in classrooms   ☐ in the rest rooms

   ☐ in hallways   ☐ in the cafeteria

   ☐ on the playground   ☐ on the school bus

6. I get bullied on my way to and from school.

   ☐ Never   ☐ Once in a while

   ☐ A lot   ☐ Every day

7. I worry about being bullied when I'm in school.

   ☐ Never   ☐ Once in a while

   ☐ A lot   ☐ Every day

8. If someone bullies me, I usually

   ☐ tell the student who bullies to stop   ☐ tell an adult at school

   ☐ tell another student   ☐ tell my parents

   ☐ don't do anything   ☐ I don't get bullied

9. If I see someone else getting bullied, I usually

   ☐ help the student who is bullied   ☐ join in the bullying

   ☐ tell an adult at school   ☐ tell another student

   ☐ tell my parents   ☐ don't do anything

10. To help me feel safe at our school, I think adults should

   ☐ make rules about bullying

   ☐ enforce rules about bullying

   ☐ teach more lessons about how to get along better

   ☐ have better supervision of the

      ☐ school bus   ☐ rest rooms

      ☐ playground   ☐ hallways

      ☐ cafeteria   ☐ classrooms

Bullying Denny

1ST ACTOR: You're such a nerd, Denny.
               Your shoes are too shiny.

2ND ACTOR: You're such a pain, Denny.
               Your voice is so whiny.

1ST ACTOR: You're such a klutz, Denny.
               You can't ride a two-wheeler.

2ND ACTOR: You're such a dweeb, Denny.
               You're also a squealer.

1ST ACTOR: I'm gonna get you right after lunch.
               And when I get you, you'll get a punch.

2ND ACTOR: I'm gonna poke you one, right in the eye.
               And laugh in your face when you start to cry.

1ST ACTOR: I might make you crawl, or better yet, dance.
               'Cause if you don't, I'll pull down your pants.

2ND ACTOR: Maybe I'll kick you hard in the tush,
               Or knock you or push you right into a bush.

BOTH: Do you know who likes you? No one, that's who.
               That's nobody, Denny. No one likes you!

Answer Key for Bullying Behaviors Word Search

The answers for the Bullying Behaviors Word Search found in the student workbook are circled in the puzzle below. Also included here is the list of words the students are to find.

```
n  l  k  e  e  p  o  u  t  p  k
w  a  b  y  l  u  s  h  u  e  m
o  u  m  e  a  n  t  r  i  c  k
d  g  l  e  k  c  w  p  u  k  l
t  h  a  s  c  h  n  s  o  t  o
u  a  f  a  h  a  t  o  n  s  o
p  t  g  e  y  e  l  l  i  n  g
s  o  y  t  a  y  e  l  t  y  r
m  i  r  l  t  a  h  k  i  c  k
o  i  s  r  e  s  t  r  i  n  o
p  h  i  t  u  p  i  s  s  o  g
r  d  i  p  r  a  l  l  t  s  o
```

dirty look	laugh at	put down
gossip	mean trick	steal
hit	name-calling	tease
keep out	punch	trip
kick	push	yelling

Power Tools

During session 7 of kindergarten and first grade and session 5 of each other level of the student curriculum of the *No-Bullying Program,* the students are introduced to new Power Tools that they can use in response to bullying. For your convenience, the complete set of Power Tools for kindergarten through eighth grade is shown below.

Introduced to Kindergartners and First-Graders

Word Power

Steps in Word Power: Make eye contact with the student who is bullying and use an I-statement while making the ASL *no/not* sign.

EXAMPLE OF WORD POWER:

STUDENT WHO BULLIES: "You are so stupid. The way you play video games is dumb."

TARGETED STUDENT: "I don't like it when you call me names, and I want you to stop."

Find a Friend

Steps in Find a Friend: Call out to nearby students, say you're being bullied, and ask them to come stand with you and make the ASL *no/not* sign.

EXAMPLE OF FIND A FRIEND:

STUDENT WHO BULLIES: "Hey, stupid, I want that ball. Give it to me if you know what's good for you."

TARGETED STUDENT: "Tyler, Melissa, Mark, I'm getting hassled. Help me out. Stand here with me and make the sign."

Run Away

Steps in Run Away: Choose a safe direction, run, and tell an adult as soon as you can.

EXAMPLE OF RUN AWAY:

STUDENT WHO BULLIES: "I'm going to wipe you off the face of the earth."

TARGETED STUDENT: Looks to see if the playground supervisor is anywhere in sight, sees her, and runs across the playground to her.

Resources

Respect & Protect®
A Practical, Step-by-Violence Prevention
and Intervention Program for School
and Communities
by Carole Remboldt and Richard Zimman
Item No. 3034

Respect & Protect® Complete Set
by Carole Remboldt and Richard Zimman
Item No. 3038

Respect & Protect® Staff Survey
Item No. 3316

Respect & Protect® VIDEO
Item No. 3037

Understanding the Human Volcano
What Teens Can Do about Violence
by Earl Hipp
Item No. 1613

The Parent's Book about Bullying
Changing the Course of Your Child's Life
by William Voors
Item No. 1231

**Why Parents Need to Know More
. . . About Bullying**
by William Voors
Item No. 1784

It's Not Only Murder VIDEO
Discovering the Violence in Your Life
Item No. 1821

It's Not Okay to Bully VIDEO
by Cordelia Anderson
Item No. 5883

Bullying
An Overview for Educators
by Beverly B. Title, Ph.D.
Item No. 1919

Violence in Schools
The Enabling Factor
by Carole Remboldt
Item No. 3035

**Solving Violence Problems in
Your School**
Why a Systematic Approach Is Necessary:
A Guide for Educators
Item No. 3036

Hazelden Information and Educational Services is a division of the Hazelden Foundation, a not-for-profit organization. Since 1949, Hazelden has been a leader in promoting the dignity and treatment of people afflicted with the disease of chemical dependency.

The mission of the foundation is to improve the quality of life for individuals, families, and communities by providing a national continuum of information, education, and recovery services that are widely accessible; to advance the field through research and training; and to improve our quality and effectiveness through continuous improvement and innovation.

Stemming from that, the mission of this division is to provide quality information and support to people wherever they may be in their personal journey—from education and early intervention, through treatment and recovery, to personal and spiritual growth.

Although our treatment programs do not necessarily use everything Hazelden publishes, our bibliotherapeutic materials support our mission and the Twelve Step philosophy upon which it is based. We encourage your comments and feedback.

The headquarters of the Hazelden Foundation are in Center City, Minnesota. Additional treatment facilities are located in Chicago, Illinois; New York, New York; Plymouth, Minnesota; St. Paul, Minnesota; and West Palm Beach, Florida. At these sites, we provide a continuum of care for men and women of all ages. Our Plymouth facility is designed specifically for youth and families.

For more information on Hazelden, please call **1-800-257-7800.** Or you may access our World Wide Web site on the Internet at **http://www.hazelden.org.**

Introduced to Second- and Third-Graders

School Rule

Steps in School Rule: Use an assertive (sure) posture and tone of voice while delivering the School Rule formula: "Our school has a rule against bullying, and _____ is breaking the rule."
      (identify bullying behavior)

EXAMPLE OF SCHOOL RULE:

STUDENT WHO BULLIES: "Hey, get out of my way, punk. I need to get my lunch."

TARGETED STUDENT: Using an assertive posture and tone of voice, says, "Our school has a rule against bullying, and cutting in line and name-calling are breaking the rule."

Introduced to Fourth- and Fifth-Graders

Skipping CD

Steps in Skipping CD: Use an assertive (sure) posture and tone of voice while delivering the Skipping CD response: "I won't let anyone bully me." Repeat the phrase in response to a new bullying behavior until the student stops bullying.

EXAMPLE OF SKIPPING CD:

STUDENT WHO BULLIES: "Hey, kid, give me your lunch money."

TARGETED STUDENT: Using an assertive posture and tone of voice, says, "I won't let anyone bully me."

STUDENT WHO BULLIES: "Hand it over!"

TARGETED STUDENT: "I won't let anyone bully me."

STUDENT WHO BULLIES: "Didn't you hear me?"

TARGETED STUDENT: "I won't let anyone bully me."

Introduced to Sixth- through Eighth-Graders

Surprise Agreement

Steps in Surprise Agreement: Use an assertive (sure) posture and tone of voice while delivering the Surprise Agreement response, which is to agree with whatever the student who bullies says. Regardless of what the student says, take him or her by surprise by agreeing.

EXAMPLE OF SURPRISE AGREEMENT:

STUDENT WHO BULLIES: "You have such class. It looks like that outfit cost you, like . . . nothing at all. Where did you get it, out of someone's garbage?"

TARGETED STUDENT: Using an assertive posture and tone of voice, says, "Yeah, it didn't cost much. That's the great part about recycling."

Leave 'Em Laughing

Steps in Leave 'Em Laughing: Use an assertive (sure) posture and tone of voice while delivering the Leave 'Em Laughing response, which is to use humor to deflect (turn away) the bullying behavior.

EXAMPLE OF LEAVE 'EM LAUGHING:

STUDENT WHO BULLIES: "Hey, kid, give me your lunch money!"

TARGETED STUDENT: Using an assertive posture and tone of voice, says, "Do you take credit cards?"